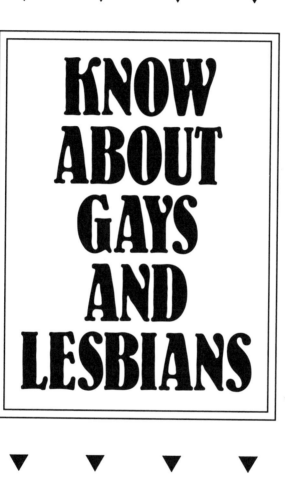

KNOW ABOUT GAYS AND LESBIANS

BY MARGARET O. HYDE AND
ELIZABETH H. FORSYTH, M.D.

The Millbrook Press
Brookfield, Connecticut

Library of Congress Cataloging-in-Publication Data
Hyde, Margaret O. (Margaret Oldroyd)
Know about gays and lesbians / Margaret O. Hyde
and Elizabeth H. Forsyth.
p.   cm.
Includes bibliographical references and index.
ISBN 1-56294-298-0 (lib. bdg.)
1. Gays—United States—Juvenile literature.   2. Homosexuality—
United States—Juvenile literature.   3. Homophobia—United
States—Juvenile literature.   4. AIDS (Disease)—Juvenile literature.
5. Gays—Family relationships—Juvenile literature.   I. Forsyth,
Elizabeth Held.   II. Title.
HQ76.26.H93   1994
305.9'0664—dc20   92-45854   CIP

Published by The Millbrook Press
2 Old New Milford Road
Brookfield, Connecticut 06804

▼ CONTENTS ▼

▼ KNOW ABOUT ▼
GAYS AND LESBIANS

▼ ONE ▼
DO YOU KNOW A GAY OR LESBIAN?

A gay or lesbian may be your best friend and you may not even know that person is homosexual. Gays and lesbians vary in age, emotional maturity, social status, financial status, personality, and many other ways. You may feel hostile or tolerant about homosexuals, or you may be an advocate for better understanding.

Prejudice against homosexuality has been called the last acceptable prejudice in the United States. While some states propose laws to make it illegal to pass legislation that would protect gays and lesbians, others pass laws that make it illegal to discriminate against them. Even some deeply religious people argue whether or not they should love their neighbors if their neighbors are gays or lesbians. The whole subject of homosexuality is shrouded in such emotionalism that many adults prefer not to think about it. Young people are more open in their search for the truth and more willing to look at both sides of a controversy, although many find gay bashing an outlet for violence that their families can accept.

In the past, almost all gays and lesbians tried to hide their true sexual orientation. A large percentage still do. Often, a young person who feels attracted to people of the same sex thinks he or she is the only one in the world who feels that way. Many young people who have some homosexual thoughts or experiences become very concerned that they are homosexual, but only a small portion of all people who have such experiences adopt male or female gay identities.[1] For those who find that they are really gay, there is a wide variation in life-styles—so much so that many scientists prefer the term "homosexualities" to "homosexuality."

A long list of slang names have been used to refer to homosexuals and to degrade them. (Homosexual men prefer to be called gays, and homosexual women prefer to be called lesbians, but sometimes these women are also referred to as gays.)

Gays and lesbians are the subject of jokes, and many are the victims of physical violence. Many of them are ignored or considered unlikable, offensive, wicked, sinful, or even criminal. Intense homophobia—the fear and dread of homosexuals and homosexuality—permeates American culture. It is virtually impossible to grow up without becoming at least somewhat homophobic. This applies to gays as well as non-gays, although many gays are happy about their lives and would not want to be straight.[2]

Myths about homosexuality abound. For example, many people confuse transvestites, men who have a compulsion to dress in women's clothing but are mainly heterosexuals, with homosexuals. Others equate all gays with pedophiles, heterosexual or homosexual adults who seek sexual satisfaction from children. Education about gays and lesbians continues to be uncommon in schools, and information about them can be difficult to obtain. But the climate is changing.

When you think of homosexuals, do you automatically picture them dressing or acting a certain way, or calling attention to themselves through sit-ins, marches, and a variety of activities that are against the law?

Just like heterosexuals, homosexuals differ enormously from one another; but many heterosexuals, especially those who think they have never met a gay or lesbian, lump all homosexuals together. They accept the stereotype of gays and lesbians as obsessed with sex, placing a narrow focus on one dimension of their life-styles. Many people object to gays because they believe the myth that they try to recruit heterosexuals to their way of life.

Like heterosexuals, homosexuals are, for the most part, loving, capable, and hardworking. Since there are as many different kinds of homosexuals as there are heterosexuals, though, some are not likable. They come from all social classes, have very different appearances, act differently, have different values, and so on. Some can be identified easily by the way they walk and talk, but many—husbands and wives, brothers and sisters—cannot be identified as homosexual even by the families with whom they live.

Although it is easy to define homosexuals as people who have sexual desires for members of the same sex, or as people who engage in sexual activities with the same sex, the subject is much more complex. Homosexual relationships can include many dimensions—emotional, intellectual, spiritual, as well as sexual.

People can't be divided into two different populations, heterosexual and homosexual. Just as everything is not black or white, many people fall in categories in between the two terms. For example, many men are exclusively heterosexual, or straight, but others are only predominantly heterosexual. They sometimes engage in homosexual feelings or acts. Some are not gay, but do have experiences with male prostitutes.

In the 1940s the researcher Alfred Kinsey and his colleagues suggested a scale for men and women that has been widely accepted. They put people in categories from zero to six. Category zero was exclusively heterosexual, category three was bisexual (both homosexual and straight), and category six was exclusively homosexual. Actually, most people do not fit neatly into these categories or pigeonholes, but this is a way of showing that there are many gradations.[3]

Even though each gay and lesbian is a different individual, environment plays a part in how they live their lives. Alex Thio, who has written a book on deviant behavior (that which deviates from the majority), divides male homosexuals into seven types, admitting that some fall into several.

One type is known as a trade homosexual. He is a well-respected married man who uses homosexual experiences as a means of relieving tension. His encounters usually take place in public restrooms, where he and his partner rarely speak to each other. They may not even know each other's names, and they have no interest in learning about the other person. Usually, the homosexual incidents occur only when there is a lack of sex at home.

Another type is a teenage runaway who earns his living by allowing older men to use him sexually. He is a street hustler, who will probably be entirely heterosexual when he is older.

Prison homosexuals are primarily heterosexuals. Their confinement dictates the gender of their sex partners. After prison, they return to a heterosexual life-style.

Male bisexuals often enjoy sexual experiences with women as much as with men, but some of them marry mainly to cover their homosexual identity. They treat their marriage partners as friends but not as sex partners.

Call boys are likely to be unmarried, have had some heterosexual experience, and enjoy their homosexual encounters. They are often very promiscuous and engage in a variety of sexual acts with customers. When they are too old to attract customers, they continue in a homosexual life-style.

So-called "closet queens" are married or unmarried men who keep their sexual orientation hidden from the public. They avoid association with known homosexuals in public, trying to pass as heterosexual even though they are predominantly or exclusively homosexual. Many homosexuals look down on this kind of person, especially today, when there is a strong movement to encourage openness and pride in homosexuality.

"Gay guys" are exclusively and openly homosexual and are part of the gay culture. Many of them form permanent love relationships with another man and live with that partner for many years, or even a lifetime. Many gay guys are working hard toward making homosexuality respectable.[4]

Although individuals may fit easily in one or more of the above groups, some don't fit well in any group. However, heterosexuals' feelings about gays are often based on knowledge of the social behavior of just one group. How do you feel about each of these types of homosexuals? Do you like some better than others?

What do you think of the practice of outing—the exposure of the sexual orientation of famous people who prefer to hide it? Activists—who include members of organizations such as Queer Nation and ACT UP, many of whom feel they need to attract attention in every possible way—are only a very small percentage of the total number of gays and lesbians. Gays and lesbians themselves disagree about the best ways to counteract the many myths about them. Most of them are still hiding, or seeking to win acceptance in ways that are not offensive to the general public.

Lesbians seem to be somewhat more acceptable to much of society than gays. When women hold hands or put their arms around each other in public, their actions seem natural, but men who show affection in public repulse many heterosexuals.

Just as there are many kinds of gays, there are many patterns of lesbian relationships. Many people still believe that all lesbians are either "butch" (masculine and aggressive) or "femme" (receptive and feminine) and that they pair together. The butch member of the partnership is supposed to initiate the lovemaking, while the femme plays the traditional female role. Today, many lesbians say that this kind of relationship, which is based on a heterosexual model, is a thing of the past. Others claim that it is one form of relationship to be explored, as long as it does not exploit the female partner.[5]

Lesbian life-styles cover a wide range. Some lesbians are sexually involved with each other, while others are just very close friends who never go beyond kissing and hugging. Some have many lovers and say they are happy with their freedom from close attachments. Others enter into a monogamous relationship. Just as in a heterosexual marriage, they work to find a healthy balance between close relationship and distance to grow as individuals.

Two women who live together are generally more accepted than two men, but many lesbians conceal their homosexuality and suffer from not being able to speak of it openly. For example, a woman whom we'll call Sharon is an executive in a large company and is careful not to let anyone know that she is a lesbian. She wishes she could keep a picture of her partner on her desk, discuss their good times together, and share experiences with her family the way heterosexuals do. She is sure there must be many lesbians working in her company, but she is afraid to let people know about her sexual orientation. If someone finds out, she is sure she will lose her job.

You probably know more about homosexuality than your parents did when they were your age. In recent years, some gays and lesbians in politics, the media, and the arts have made their preferences public. Gays have also gained attention in the age of AIDS (acquired immune deficiency syndrome), a disease that has hit the homosexual community especially hard. Although AIDS has brought some negative publicity, it has also helped to educate.

As new organizations work to help people with AIDS, they help develop greater acceptance and understanding of gays and lesbians. Gay presses are publishing books that make their way into public and school libraries. Many religious groups are discussing new attitudes toward homosexuality, and some are speaking out for "equal treatment of all of God's children."

Some large business firms, the American Bar Association, the American Medical Association, and many other organizations have been supportive with positive statements and resolutions. The American Federation of Teachers and the National Education Association have denounced discrimination against lesbian and gay teachers.[6] Even before his inauguration in 1993, President Bill Clinton announced that he planned to lift the ban on homosexuals in the military. While gays rejoiced, many others were angry because they felt this challenged a strong tradition, would create discipline problems, and would expose heterosexuals to advances from gays. It would be the most radical change in the military since President Harry S. Truman ordered the Army integrated in 1948.[7] In the end, opposition to the change forced a compromise in which homosexuals could serve if they kept their sexual preferences to themselves.

Even though the climate is changing, most gays and lesbians still live in a hostile environment, where only a relatively few voices speak out for them. Much stigma remains. Consider the following example of a typical reaction to a gay high school student.

Alison and her friends enjoyed making fun of a boy in their class who swished—walked more like a girl than a boy. They called him many different names, often when he was close enough to hear them. One day, Alison's brother asked her to stop "bashing" the boy. He told her that he had some very macho-looking gay friends on his basketball team and that not all effeminate boys are gay. Her brother talked to her about hurting people's feelings by name-calling, and she passed his message to her friends. Some of them listened to her, but many continued the name-calling.

In Alison's class, feelings about gays and lesbians ranged from acceptance to ridicule and hate. Many of the students were uncomfortable when talking about any kind of sex, although they liked to tell dirty jokes to each other.[8] Some members of the class thought they might be gay themselves, and they pretended that they believed homosexuality was wrong so that no one would suspect their true feelings. Others became more tolerant of homosexuals, but some continued to feel gays were weird, sick, or just abnormal.

Suppose there are thirty people in your class. Chances are good that one or more of them are gay or lesbian. You may know them well and still have no idea of their sexual orientation. You probably know many more homosexuals without realizing it.

The estimates of the incidence of homosexuality range from 1 percent to 10 percent of the population. Most recent studies give a range of figures for the incidence of gays and lesbians, since various definitions are used. Getting a true answer to questions about something people do not want known makes research difficult.[9] Of the estimated 29 million adolescents, nearly 3 million are probably gay.[10]

Even if the lowest estimate of homosexuality—1 percent—is correct, this is still a large number. One percent of the teenage and voting population is more than the populations of Vermont and New Hampshire combined.

Do you suppose any of your friends is gay or lesbian? You may feel certain that you do not know any homosexuals because none of your friends has approached you with actions that would indicate they were interested in any kind of sexual relationship.

Many gays never admit their feelings to any of their friends. The idea that homosexuals try to have sex with just anyone is far from true. You may well know many people who hide their sexual orientation.

Many people of all ages believe they do not know any homosexuals, for they think they can spot all gays and lesbians by the way they talk, walk, dress, act, or look. This may be true in some cases, but as Alison learned, it is not always so. Many adults believe people are either entirely homosexual or straight, although they do hear about a bisexual once in a while. They do not realize that there are homosexuals among all kinds of professions and occupations. They may be rich or poor, handsome or plain, intelligent or stupid, friendly or shy, or any gradation in between. This holds true for women and for men. Some gays are great athletes, executives, doctors, or dancers. So are some lesbians. So are some heterosexuals.

Many people are shocked to find that gay youths have an attempted suicide rate between two and three and a half times greater than other youths.[11] The Report of the Secretary's Task Force on Youth Suicide, which appeared in January 1989, explains that the homosexual risk factor stems from the effects of hostility against gays, not from the homosexuality itself. Many otherwise caring people contribute to this because they do not know better. You need not be one of them.

Certainly, many gays and lesbians live productive and meaningful lives. Most of them want what heterosexuals want: to be accepted by their families and friends, to share their lives with loving companions, to participate in their places of worship and communities, and to have the same rights as other citizens of their country. Most of them are happy with their life-styles, and like heterosexuals, each one is different.

▼ TWO ▼
HIDDEN HISTORY

The study of sexual behavior has long been hindered by prejudice, prudery, taboos, misconceptions, and a conspiracy of silence. Even physicians have difficulty in dealing with sexual matters. At a meeting of the American Medical Association in 1899, when Dr. Denslow Lewis attempted to present a paper concerning the "hygiene of the sexual act," another physician objected because "discussion of the subject is attended with filth and we besmirch ourselves by discussing it in public." [1] One British writer of the nineteenth century thought that the books by male and female authors should be properly separated on people's bookshelves, unless the authors happened to be married to each other.

If sex between men and women is a forbidden topic, then any mention of homosexuality makes some people even more uncomfortable. Even in the twentieth century, some college professors told their students to omit translating passages in Greek and Latin literature that contained references to "Greek love" or other unmentionable sexual activities. In fact, most histories of Greece written before 1950 do not even contain any references to homosexuality.[2] In 1871, when British scholar John Addington Symonds wrote what was probably the first history of Greek homosexuality, he published only ten copies of the study because he feared prosecution by the British government.[3] Now, more than a hundred years later, there are still many missing pieces of information in the study of gay and lesbian history. Even less has been written about lesbians than about gays.

Homosexuality has been called a sin, an unspeakable vice, a crime against nature, an inherited form of degeneracy, and a psychological disorder. Despite the fact that there have been many recent advances in the study of homosexuality by anthropologists, sociologists, historians, psychologists, and psychiatrists, some people still hold preconceived notions. For instance, there is a mistaken belief that homosexual behavior is unusual in most societies and that it is always condemned when it occurs. But it has not always been considered sinful, perverse, or criminal. Same-sex activity occurred in ancient China, Japan, and in the Islamic world as well as in Greece. In the ancient world, people were not usually divided into heterosexual or homosexual categories, as they are today.

The ancient Greeks had no words for homosexuality or heterosexuality; they took it for granted that an adult male could be attracted by beauty in either sex.[4] In the classical era of Greece, sexual intercourse was not a mutual activity between two equals. The active partner was dominant, and the passive partner could be either male or female. It was acceptable for an upper-class adult male Athenian to have sexual relations with women, boys, slaves, or foreigners, all of whom were considered subordinate. In other words, a man who engaged in these same-sex activities was not given a special label.

The practice of pederasty, or sexual relationships between males of unequal ages, can be documented at least as far back as 800 B.C. among the ancient Greeks. The custom of an older man becoming a mentor or teacher to a younger man is thought to have originated as part of an initiation rite for young men. Pederasty may even have begun in the Stone Age, stemming from the ancient belief that semen was a powerful life-force.[5] In our society, sex—heterosexual or homosexual—between a teacher and student is generally condemned. But this practice was a normal part of development among the Greeks; the boys went on to normal adulthood and marriage, and then might become mentors themselves.

The Greeks recognized that some men were different because they preferred men exclusively. However, these relationships between adults of the same sex and age were not considered acceptable, and were often ridiculed. In the second century A.D., the Greek physician Soranus wrote about soft or unmasculine men (called *molles* by the Roman translator) who acted and dressed like women, and who preferred the passive or receptive role in intercourse. He also described women (called *tri-bades*) who preferred sex with other women. This condition was thought to be caused by a mental disease brought on by excessive sexual desire.[6]

Not much is known about female homosexuality among the ancient Greeks, but the most famous example is the poet Sappho, whose poetry clearly reflected her erotic feelings for women. The modern term "lesbian" is derived from the name of the island of Lesbos, where she lived in the sixth century B.C. Most of Sappho's writings were destroyed later by the Christians because of their homosexual content.

According to sociologist David F. Greenberg, most ancient societies except for the Egyptians and the Hebrews permitted some forms of homosexuality.[7] Among societies in the modern world, there are many non-Western tribal groups in which same-sex activity is practiced. Although many disapprove of adult homosexuality, most non-Western cultures have been more tolerant of homosexual behavior than is our society. In a famous study, published in 1951, researchers Clellan Ford and Frank Beach found that homosexual behavior was socially acceptable or normal for certain people in 64 percent of seventy-six cultures.[8]

Transgenerational homosexual activity (that is, between males of unequal ages) is known to exist in Africa, South America, New Guinea, and other places. Among the Sambia of New Guinea, boys traditionally entered into prescribed homosexual relationships, which lasted for many years, until they married or became fathers.[9] Like the Greek student-mentor relationships, this kind of same-sex activity does not exist in our society.

In a few societies, the custom of adopting opposite sex-roles is practiced. Cross-dressing (also called transgenderal homosexuality) involves taking on the sexual identity of the other sex. The best-known examples have been found in many North American Indian tribes.[10] The early Spanish and French explorers and missionaries wrote about Indian men who wore women's clothing, married other men, and engaged in women's occupations. They were called *berdaches* by the French. There were also females who became berdaches, adopting men's clothing and sometimes joining men in hunting and going to war.

The gender change was not necessarily complete or lasting. Some berdaches did not take on all the characteristic behavior or clothing of the opposite sex. There is some disagreement among writers as to whether or not the role was always permanent, once it was taken on. Some berdaches had both heterosexual and homosexual relationships, while others were celibate.

Sometimes parents interpreted certain behavior in a child as a sign that the child should be raised as a member of the opposite sex. In other cases, an adult man or woman might have a dream or vision directing him or her to become a berdache.

Acceptance of berdaches varied, perhaps due in part to the extent to which the various tribes were influenced by the disapproval of European missionaries. However, berdaches were generally not disapproved of, but on the contrary were often revered as healers or spiritual leaders.

It is clear that many different modern and ancient societies throughout the world have accepted some forms of same-sex activity. But in Western society, changes in attitude began to occur during the time of the ancient Greeks.

There was a gradual shift toward more restraint in sexual behavior, and Greek acceptance of male homosexuality began to wane around the fourth century B.C.[11] Plato thought that pederasty between students and teachers could be justified if it helped the learning process, but he later wrote that sex should be reserved for marriage and procreation.

Some of the early Christians believed that sex was sinful and rejected it altogether, demanding complete abstinence, even between married couples. Saint Augustine, however, believed that sex in marriage without lust was permissible if it led to procreation. Any intercourse not intended for the purpose of having children was forbidden; it followed that homosexuality was forbidden.

During the Middle Ages, it was common knowledge that homosexuality was widespread, even in monasteries and convents. According to some writers, the attitude toward homosexuals was rather lenient in the early Middle Ages, until about the twelfth century.[12] But from then on, until the nineteenth century, the practice continued to be condemned as a sin and crime against nature, both in Europe and the New World. Although the penalties were very severe—hanging, stoning, castration, or dismemberment—the harsh measures did not deter these practices. In fact, there were established social networks of homosexuals in the cities.[13] Writers in the fourteenth and fifteenth centuries complained that Italian cities such as Bologna, Florence, and Venice were "infested" with homosexuality. The laws were not always strictly or uniformly enforced, probably because the elite were engaging in the same behavior.

Among those who engaged in homosexual activities were some well-known artists, for example, Leonardo da Vinci and Michelangelo, each of whom took younger lovers. It was customary for many adult males to consider boys interchangeable with women.

Although homosexuality in women was recognized and condemned as a sin in medieval and early modern times, it never received much attention, in part because people thought women could not satisfy each other sexually. There was much disagreement about the meaning of terms and confusion about how lesbian practices fit into the definition of sodomy (sodomy was generally defined as anal intercourse between males). Authorities also disagreed about the seriousness of the crime.

Some believed that female sodomy was such a monstrous act that they called it the "silent sin." It was thought to be worse than male sodomy and not fit to be named or written. One authority recommended that when judgment was pronounced against a woman convicted of sodomy, a description of the crime should not be read aloud, as was the usual custom. Women were considered weaker by nature, therefore more suggestible, so it was feared that merely hearing of such activities might arouse their desire.[14] In cases where one partner dressed as a male, the punishment was generally more severe for that partner, because there was greater disapproval of a woman who dared to deviate from her traditional role to take over the function of a man.

Beginning in about 1700, some changes occurred that signaled the beginnings of modern attitudes toward homosexuality. Before the modern era, homosexuality was considered an activity in which anyone theoretically might engage. The term referred to behavior, not to sexual identity or orientation.

Gradually, there was a shift in attitudes. People began to view homosexuality as a deviant activity practiced by a small number of effeminate males. Such men became known as fops in England. They were also called "mollies," and later were known as "queens."

Groups of men who were exclusively homosexual began to gather at clubs and meeting places called molly houses in England. The molly houses were raided periodically by the authorities, and their patrons were prosecuted. Similar groups formed social networks in other countries. In Amsterdam, in 1730, three hundred men were prosecuted for the crime of homosexuality and seventy were executed.[15]

Many leading thinkers of the eighteenth and nineteenth centuries began to echo some new ideas that were arising, among them the notion that human behavior is governed by natural laws. They argued that homosexuality was not harmful and should not be punished. In France, same-sex activity between consenting adults was legal under the Penal Code of 1791 and the Napoleonic Code of 1810. Still, although the French law spread to many other countries, homosexuals continued to be prosecuted and harassed in France and elsewhere. It was not until 1861 that the death penalty for homosexuality was repealed in England.

In the nineteenth and twentieth centuries, much change occurred. Although many gays and lesbians continued to hide their sexual orientation, and discrimination continued in many forms, a movement toward openness, or "coming out of the closet," began.

▼ THREE ▼
OUT OF THE CLOSET

By the nineteenth century there was an established gay underground, but opposition and prejudice continued. In fact, until the second half of the twentieth century, every state of the United States still retained old laws against sodomy, which included some heterosexual as well as homosexual acts.

Scientists of the nineteenth century became interested in finding the causes of homosexuality. The idea that homosexuality was inborn "inverted sexual instinct" gained popularity. It was thought to be due to hereditary factors or a predisposition that might be brought out by such activities as masturbation or reading dirty books. Richard von Krafft-Ebing was the most influential of the early researchers who believed that hereditary defects were the chief cause of sexual perversions.[1] Sexual activity with someone of the same sex was classified as only one of a number of so-called sexual inversions. In 1892, Charles Gilbert Craddock translated a German term and introduced the word homosexuality into the English language. However, the term did not come into general use until much later, and it was not even included in the *Oxford English Dictionary* until 1976.

Krafft-Ebing and other medical authorities believed that people who suffered from these defects should not be punished as criminals, but should be treated in mental institutions. Any behavior that did not follow the culturally approved standards for one's gender role was considered a sexual inversion. One late-nineteenth-century author blamed the increase of homosexuality in women on their increasing independence from men and their pursuit of careers.[2] In a 1907 article in the *New York Medical Journal,* Dr. Ralph W. Parsons warned that education for women was dangerous to their constitutions and would make them more masculine. As late as 1920, one expert wrote that political aspirations in women and a fondness for cats in men were signs of inversion.

A number of women in the nineteenth century and earlier passed as men by cross-dressing and adopting male mannerisms and speech. They did this because they wanted to better their economic status, to gain more social and sexual independence, or to seek adventure. Some of the cross-dressers were feminists, but most feminists did not wear men's clothing. In the late nineteenth century, there were women who went out in public wearing some items of men's clothing. The medical profession associated this cross-dressing with sexual inversion, and these women were known as "mannish lesbians." (In present-day terminology, they would be called "butch.") The British author Radclyffe Hall, who was a declared lesbian, wrote a novel called *The Well of Loneliness* that was published in 1928. Although the book was criticized by later feminists for the way it portrayed lesbians, it was significant because it broke the silence and became the most widely read book of its time that dealt with homosexual relationships between women.

In the Victorian era, people thought that only men and lower-class women had sexual desires, so it was natural for them to think that all lesbians identified with men. Numerous intense, romantic friendships sprang up between middle-class women in this era, and many female couples lived together for years; some of these relationships were sexual and some were not. There is disagreement among present-day scholars as to whether or not these women should be characterized as lesbians.[3] As noted earlier, affectionate behavior between women has always been regarded as acceptable, whereas the same behavior between two men would be looked on with suspicion.

Just as not every lesbian is "mannish," not every gay is effeminate. Consider this account of an investigation carried out by the United States Navy during the years of 1919 and 1920. Its purpose was to uncover the "immoral conditions" in the community of Newport, Rhode Island, where the Newport Naval Training Station was located. There was a gay subculture in Newport, and many of its members were sailors.[4]

The Navy sent a number of enlisted men to act as decoys to entrap suspected "sexual perverts" and have sex with them. From their testimony during the hearings, a good picture of this gay community emerged. Relatively few of the men who engaged in homosexual behavior were considered by others or by themselves as different from other men solely on that basis. Rather, the important factor was the gender role that the man assumed. Those who acted effeminate and showed other "feminine" characteristics—gestures, expressions, or walk, for example—were referred to (by themselves and others) as "queers." They took the passive or traditional female role in sexual relations. When they were off duty, some (known as "queens") dressed in women's clothing (in drag), took women's names, and gave parties to which both straight and gay men were invited. It was obvious that the "queers" constituted a group that was different.

In contrast, there was another group of men who engaged in homosexual activities, and their sexual identity was not as clear-cut. Some were married to women. They conformed to the traditional masculine gender role; they never acted effeminate or cross-dressed, and they never took the female or passive role during sexual activity. Some entered into steady relationships with "queers" and were referred to as "husbands." As a result of the investigation, several dozen sailors and civilians were arrested.

At first, the behavior of heterosexual men who had occasional sexual encounters with "queers" was not questioned, and the Navy did not prosecute them. Many of the heterosexual men involved openly admitted their involvement in this kind of homosexual activity, in which the masculine and feminine roles were clearly defined. Neither they themselves nor the Navy regarded them as "perverted."

At the start of the investigation, the Navy took it for granted that the decoys were "straight," and they were never asked to assume the role of "queer." Some members of the so-called "pervert squad" even received commendations for their "interest and zeal in this work."[5] But as the hearings progressed, it became evident that some of the decoys had enjoyed their sexual encounters, and in some cases had initiated the contacts with suspected "perverts." The boundaries between "straight" and "perverted" began to blur, and distinguishing between them was not an easy matter. If the decoys could be implicated, then the investigators realized that they would have to prosecute many men who previously had been considered straight. After some controversy and an inquiry by the Senate Naval Affairs Committee regarding the methods used in gathering evidence, the Navy backed off from further pursuit and pardoned some of the men who had been convicted.

In the 1920s and 1930s, there was continued suppression of homosexuality; the attempt to root out perversion in the Navy was only one example. Books and movies were subjected to censorship of objectionable material. History was rewritten to conform with traditional values when a 1933 movie about the lesbian Queen Christina of Sweden depicted her as marrying a Spanish ambassador.[6]

Sexual nonconformity was accepted among the artists and intellectuals of the black entertainment world that flourished in New York City's Harlem section during the Jazz Age in the 1920s and early 1930s. Some of the black entertainers pretended to be heterosexual in their public life, but were homosexual or bisexual. Many white homosexuals found that they too were tolerated in these circles. There was a feeling of identification and kinship between these groups that were not in the mainstream of society. According to one writer, this phenomenon may have been the beginning of a homosexual "minority consciousness."

During the same era in Germany, much of the early research into sexual behavior was being carried on by a number of scientists, most of whom were Jewish.[7] With the rise of the Nazi movement came anti-intellectualism, anti-Semitism, and homophobia. Scholarly research into sexual matters and psychoanalysis were called "Jewish science" and denounced. Within months after Hitler became chancellor of Germany in 1933, a prestigious institute for sexual research in Munich was completely destroyed by the Nazis. "Sexual degenerates," a category that included homosexuals, transvestites, pimps, and "race defilers" (Jews and non-Jews) were sent along with other undesirables to concentration camps, where millions of people were exterminated. In the camps, homosexuals were near the bottom of the prisoner hierarchy, and were often singled out for torture and "medical experimentation."

Male homosexuality remained a crime in Germany after World War II, so that homosexuals who had been inmates of concentration camps did not receive compensation, as other survivors did. In fact, some were still prosecuted and imprisoned after the war under the old law, which was not repealed until the 1960s.

The first formally organized gay movement group in the United States was the Society for Human Rights, founded in 1924. But World War II marked the turning point for the emergence of a gay political movement.

Organizations such as the Mattachine Society and the Daughters of Bilitis sprang up and worked to fight discrimination and to educate people. Many of the early homosexual groups had to take ambiguous or vague names for protection, and because the telephone directory would not carry any listing with "homosexual" in its title until the late 1960s.[8]

During the Cold War in the 1950s, there was a general fear of Communist infiltration into every sphere of American life; the entertainment industry, universities, and government were all subjects of investigation. Many people lost their jobs in the campaign that was carried out under the auspices of Senator Joseph McCarthy and the United States House Committee on Un-American Activities. Because homosexuality was linked with Communism and subversion of the American way of life, many homosexuals also were eliminated from government jobs.

Homosexual relations were still considered a felony in every state during the 1950s. Although the laws were not invoked very often, one man convicted in Idaho during that period was sentenced to life imprisonment. A turning point was reached in 1961, with the Illinois Model Penal Code serving as an example for other states to decriminalize same-sex relations between consenting adults. However, as of 1993, twenty-three states still retained some form of old antisodomy laws.

Despite legal restraints, attitudes were changing in the 1960s. Gender stereotypes began to crumble. There was more sexual freedom and less opposition to divorce, premarital sex, contraception, and abortion.

The Stonewall Riot of 1969 is considered the event that ushered in a new era of changing attitudes toward homosexuals. It started when police raided a gay bar, the Stonewall Inn, in New York's Greenwich Village, and community members joined the patrons of the bar in fighting back. The changes that occurred after Stonewall were helped by the civil rights and black power movements, which served as models for gay activists. Gays also received support from the activists of the New Left reform movement and from women's liberation groups. Many gays and lesbians came out of the closet, banded together, and formed groups like the Gay Liberation Front. As the movement grew, more aggressive tactics, such as strikes and boycotts, were used. Gay groups were formed within formerly straight organizations such as the American Civil Liberties Union. Although prejudice against gays and lesbians was not eliminated, the struggle was now out in the open.

A major victory was won in 1973, when the American Psychiatric Association decided to remove homosexuality as a diagnosis of mental illness, even though many psychiatrists were opposed. Some still believe that it should be classified as a disorder. However, many psychiatrists view same-sex activity as behavior that can occur in a wide variety of emotional and life conditions. It can have different meanings and implications depending on the situation. Experts agree that a large percentage of people have had both heterosexual and homosexual experiences at some time in their lives. Psychiatrists no longer think that homosexuals should be subjected to nineteenth-century methods of treatment in efforts to force a "cure." New research suggesting a biological basis for homosexuality, discussed in the following chapter, may answer some questions but also present new problems.

▼ FOUR ▼
WHY HOMOSEXUAL OR HETEROSEXUAL?

Over the years, homosexuality has been considered a crime, a physical weakness, a moral
weakness, a mental disorder, and a normal kind
of sexual orientation. Today, opinions are still found
that fit any one of these descriptions. People continue to ask, "Are gays and lesbians born or bred
that way?"

Many researchers agree that the exact causes
of homosexuality and heterosexuality are unknown. Heterosexuals do not seem to care why
they are attracted to the opposite sex, and many
homosexuals do not care why they are attracted to
people of same sex. They just are. However, numerous studies have been made in search of the
possible causes of homosexuality. The subject
seems important to some gays and lesbians, who
feel that such knowledge would help them to gain
acceptance. It also seems important to those who
feel homosexuals are dangerous, unnatural, or
sinful. Many people are just curious.

Parents usually do much soul-searching when their sons and daughters tell them they are homosexual, trying to find what they may have done wrong. Even those who know that their adult children live happy, fulfilled lives worry about AIDS. Although their sons and daughters may now live in monogamous relationships, just as many heterosexuals do, parents worry about possible exposure to AIDS at some earlier date.

Sigmund Freud, the founder of psychoanalysis, did not believe that homosexuality was a mental illness, nor did he see much prospect for converting homosexuals into heterosexuals. However, he stopped short of developing a theory of healthful homosexuality. Through the years, psychoanalysts and psychiatrists tried to cure their homosexual patients, and as mentioned earlier it was not until 1973 that homosexuality was removed from the list of diagnostic categories as a mental illness.[1]

Today, young psychiatrists are taught to make their homosexual patients comfortable in a world that stigmatizes and discriminates against them. Doctors find that many of their patients are healthy individuals who have developed problems because of the high degree of prejudice to which they have been exposed. Rather than try to change homosexuals, liberal social scientists, psychologists, psychiatrists, and many educated people feel that it is more important to enlighten the people around them. This attitude is not accepted by many straight people, who still feel that homosexuality is a disease, a sin, or both.

The partners in a homosexual relationship, as in a heterosexual relationship, may or may not have psychological problems. Classifying homosexuality as a sickness, or disorder, has been compared with classifying left-handedness as a disorder, a common practice in schools a half century ago.[2] Some left-handed people who lived long ago were stigmatized as witches. Today, no one thinks of left-handed people as evil or sick.

A popular explanation for the cause of homosexuality has been family relationships. For many years, doctors, psychologists, and others attributed gay feelings in males to the way they were raised as children. Perry is a typical example. When he was young, Perry's mother relied on him for many of her emotional needs, and although he felt close to her, Perry knew that she was a domineering woman. His father was cold, not very involved with his son, and away from home for weeks at a time because of his business.

Perry did not share his father's interest in football, wrestling, and other "manly" sports. He was musical, like his mother, and he hated sports. Perry felt that his father rejected him, and to some degree this was true. Many of his classmates called him a sissy. Perry fit the description of the "Sissyboy Syndrome," a name many people use when they refer to homosexuals. However, many homosexuals do not fit this picture. Studies indicate that there are many so-called sissy boys who grow up to be heterosexual, and many masculine types who are homosexual.[3]

Whether or not a family situation in which there is a weak father and a dominant mother has an effect on sexual orientation is a subject of controversy, although much evidence indicates this alone is not a cause.[4]

Another subject that is controversial is the effect of parents who wish their child had been a different sex. In some cases, encouraging a girl to play rough sports or a boy to play house, hopscotch, or other girls' activities, appears to affect sexual orientation, but not everyone agrees about the influence this has. Suppose a mother wanted a girl after having three boys; but once more, her baby was a boy. She dressed him in pink until he was two years old, encouraged him to play with dolls, and protected him from any rough-and-tumble treatment. She kept his hair long in the days when only girls wore their hair this way, and she told him how much she wished he had been a girl. This son acted like a sissy, and when he grew up and discovered that he was gay, he blamed it on the way his mother raised him.[5]

There have been fewer studies about why some girls are lesbians than about why some boys are gay. Encouraging a girl to be a tomboy probably has little to do with her sexual orientation as a woman. Many lesbians are interested in boys' sports when they are growing up, but many heterosexual girls are, too.

In any case, homosexuality, both male and female, may be as deeply ingrained as heterosexuality, and differences in early experiences may reflect or express, rather than cause, eventual orientation. Many experts suggest that genes act in concert with environment.[6]

Still, many people believe that gays can change to become heterosexual. Doctors who are convinced that homosexuality is learned behavior feel that it can be unlearned. "Gays CAN change" is a controversial message that is being spread across some college campuses by leaders and students who believe that homosexuality is a wrong choice. They believe it may be the result of factors such as lack of positive role models, sexual assaults, an insatiable need for affection and attention, and discomfort with one's own body. Exodus International is an organization that offers leadership to groups who encourage such change.

Sometimes student controversy explodes into gay bashing and strong expressions of sentiment. For example, *Peninsula,* a publication written by students of Harvard University, devoted almost an entire issue to denouncing the homosexual "lifestyle" which they believed could be "bad for society" and could "destroy individuals emotionally, physically, and spiritually." [7] These college students, as well as people from all walks of life, insist that homosexuality is a matter of choice.

Homosexuals Anonymous is a Christian fellowship of men and women who have chosen to help each other live a life "free from homosexuality." There are about fifty chapters of this organization in the United States, Canada, and Australia, many of which meet weekly. They suggest options for those who live as gays and are distressed about it, and they offer free materials to anyone who wishes help in trying to change from gay to straight through counseling and group support.

Homosexuals Anonymous leaders contend that homosexuality is abnormal and is a defensive attachment to people of the same sex, an opinion that is disputed by many scientists. Their program is based on principles somewhat similar to those of Alcoholics Anonymous. Many of the leaders believe that there are no true homosexuals, that God created all people as heterosexuals. They believe that freedom from homosexuality can come to those who try hard enough to change, but they admit that changing is a long and difficult process.

Can boys and girls who are really heterosexual be pushed into homosexuality by exposure to homosexual role models? If a scout leader were discovered to be gay, would some of the boys who admired him grow up to be gay? Many parents express concern about the influence of homosexual teachers and others who are role models for their children.

Homosexuality is not contagious. The parents of homosexuals are heterosexual, and children raised by gays or lesbians are no more likely to be homosexual than those raised by heterosexuals. Homosexual role models do not cause homosexuality in others.

Suppose a boy or girl is seduced by a person of the same sex. Might this cause the young person to become a homosexual? Most gays are opposed to child molesting, just as most heterosexuals are. Child molesters are pedophiles, people who are sexually attracted to children, and they may be heterosexual or homosexual.[8] Sexual abuse of children is most common among relatives. Although such an experience may result in serious emotional problems, it is not a cause of homosexuality.

The true causes of homosexuality are still unknown. There may be many contributing factors. In December 1991, the *Archives of General Psychiatry* published the results of a study by Michael

Bailey of Northwestern University and Richard Pillard of Boston University School of Medicine on twins and homosexuality. They found that identical twins—twins who are the product of a single fertilized egg that splits in the womb—were most likely to both be gay. Of the identical twins in the study, 52 percent of the gay men had twin brothers who were also gay. Of the fraternal twins—twins who develop simultaneously from two separate fertilized eggs—the percentage was 22. Only 11 percent of the unrelated brothers—those who were adopted children—were both gay. According to one of the researchers, their work adds to the evidence that sexual orientation does not result from a moral defect.[9]

The biology of homosexuality caused a stir when results of another study made the headlines in many popular publications in early 1992. Simon LeVay, a biologist at San Diego's Salk Institute for Biological Studies, discovered a difference in a tiny part of the brains of homosexual and heterosexual male cadavers. In his study of forty-one brains taken from people who died before they were sixty years old, careful examination of a tiny node deep in a part of the brain known as the hypothalamus showed that the node was about one-quarter to one-half smaller in homosexual men than in heterosexual men. This area was known to be smaller in heterosexual women than in heterosexual men, and it is an area known to be involved in regulating sexual behavior.[10] LeVay does not claim to have found a biological cause of homosexuality, but he believes that his discovery is worth further investigation. His study's main purpose was to show that it is possible to analyze sexual orientation at the biological level.

In 1993, more studies showing a link between genetic factors and homosexuality were widely reported in the press. Many people welcomed the idea that homosexuality might have a biological basis. Parents would no longer be made to feel that they had caused homosexuality because they had a poor relationship with their children. Would a biological explanation of gayness mean that people would no longer feel the need to punish homosexuals or try to change them through therapy? Perhaps some individuals who believe gays choose to be immoral, or that they should be "cured," would change their views and accept homosexuality as a part of normal living. However, others would probably continue to feel that homosexuality is not acceptable.

The new research on possible biological causes worries some homosexuals. They fear that someday it may be possible to discover a child's sexual orientation before birth, and that this may cause parents who fear and hate homosexuals to abort their fetuses. Or embryos might be injected with hormones to produce heterosexual children.

Just as other minority groups have been hassled through the years, homosexuals have been rejected, discriminated against, and abused. Many of them still are. Evelyn Hooker, who found that it is impossible to distinguish homosexuals from heterosexuals in psychological tests as long ago as 1950, believed the issue is not what causes sexual orientation, but the reaction of heterosexuals to it. Many people agree with her.

▼ FIVE ▼
STRIVING FOR ACCEPTANCE

Do you find homosexuals offensive? Perhaps you prefer to avoid them. You may have heard jokes and unpleasant remarks about "queers" as long as you can remember, and these may have colored your feelings. Or perhaps you have strong religious convictions against gays and lesbians because you believe they live in sin. Maybe you just don't like them, without being sure why. Or perhaps you hate homosexuals because of the way some of them act. How would you feel if you found out that your best friend is gay?

Jill is a sixteen-year-old who prides herself on loving everybody, but when she is asked about gays and lesbians, she replies, "I don't like homosexuals. I wish they would keep their dirty secrets to themselves." Jill was brought up to love her neighbors, be fair, and respect the rights of other human beings. She is well known for coming to the defense of the black students in her school when they are victims of prejudice.

Jill's parents often talked openly about the "terrible" homosexuals they knew, and made unflattering remarks about people who might be hiding their homosexuality. Their parents had done the same. Jill agreed with the preachers and politicians who said that AIDS was a punishment from God. She had no answer for her friends when they asked her about the fact that, worldwide, women account for 40 percent of those infected with HIV, the AIDS virus.[1] She never thought about the large number of children who are being infected through blood transfusions in developing countries where blood is not screened. Jill's teacher pointed out that the world is handicapped in its battle against AIDS by people who think it is a homosexual disease and feel that homosexuals do not deserve treatment. Although Jill changed her opinion about the need for AIDS research, she did not feel comfortable about the subject of homosexuality. Jill hoped she would never meet a homosexual. She did not realize that a few of her close friends were same-sex oriented. They hid this information, because they wanted to be accepted by people like Jill.

Jill, along with a great many people, suffered from homophobia, an intense irrational fear of gays that is born of ignorance. Dislike of homosexuals is based on reasons ranging from objections to activists who invade churches and private places to the mistaken belief that all child molesters are homosexuals, or vice versa. The fear and intolerance are expressed both socially and personally.[2] Such attitudes can lead people to take extraordinary steps to exclude homosexuals from society or to pressure them to change.

For some men and women, counseling, extensive therapy, and religious help appear to have been successful in bringing about the change that they, or others, want. For many homosexuals, all such efforts have failed. This was the case with Justin (not his real name), a minister who suffered from the homophobia in his congregation. Justin was much loved by members of his congregation and by his wife and five children—but this was only true when his secret was well hidden.

After someone saw Justin at a gay bar with a young man who was known to be a homosexual, there was a great deal of gossip among church members. Even friends who admired him greatly talked freely in negative terms about him. When asked if he was bisexual, Justin told the truth. He was asked to leave either his lover or his church. Justin's wife and many church members pleaded with him to change his sexual orientation. Many of them believed he had chosen to be gay and would choose to give up his lover, be true to his wife, and continue with his work in the church.

Justin knew that his true feelings for his lover were much stronger than those for his wife or the people in his congregation who could not accept his homosexuality. Although he was willing to separate from them, he knew religion would always be a major part of his life. He was upset about the problems caused by his bisexuality, and he hoped that education would help the people who despised him, even though they considered themselves good Christians.

For the sake of his family, Justin wished he could change how he felt, but he knew that he did not make a conscious choice to be attracted to his lover. The feeling came from inside. Although Justin did attempt to change through therapy, he could not. Even his therapist admitted that curing his homosexual feelings was as unlikely as curing his desire to help other people.

Jill and Justin represent two sides of the problem of homophobia. Although the problem is lessening in some parts of society, it remains strong in others, including the religious community.

The subject of homosexuality causes tremendous controversy in many religious groups. These feelings run deep, and many faiths are in turmoil about whether or not homosexuals are sinners, may be ordained as leaders in the church, or be accepted only if they refrain from sex.

Many Jews and Christians cite several passages in the Bible that they believe show homosexual relations to be sinful. Theologians and scholars who have studied the Bible for many years in efforts to learn its true meaning have a variety of opinions about how these passages relate to homosexuals. They tell us that, in some cases, an ancient word may have as many as forty different meanings.

Most biblical scholars now question the interpretation of many references that are used to justify negative judgments on same-sex orientation.[3] Some controversial passages that are used to condemn homosexual acts deal with sexual behavior that is unloving and exploitive, such as prostitution. Even here, the Bible's message is one of forgiveness and healing.

Historically, biblical passages have been used

to justify slavery, the inferiority of women, and the persecution of religious minorities. Many people who interpret the scriptures literally insist that homosexuals are sinners. For example, in June 1992, two congregations were banished by Southern Baptists for accepting homosexuals, saying "their actions were contrary to the teaching of the Bible on human sexuality and sanctity of the family and are offensive to Southern Baptists." One church had blessed a homosexual union, and the other had licensed a homosexual to preach.[4]

An increasing number of religious people agree that a few passages cannot override Jesus's central message of love and reconciliation. Christianity is not a cause; it is a way of life. They feel that the Bible should not be used to try to convince people that their way is right or wrong. The purpose of the Bible is not to prove something. It is a love story, teaching people to love one another.

Many religious people accept homosexuals as church members because they believe that God forgives sins, including heterosexual sins such as child abuse, incest, adultery, and so on. Many conservative churches have welcomed homosexuals who have given up their life-styles and repented of their sins. Still others are willing to support groups of homosexuals who consider themselves normal. Acceptance of homosexual unions and leadership is less widespread, but it does exist.

Religion is an important part of the lives of many gays and lesbians, but some continue to hide their true sexual identity. Many who talked to their church leaders about their feelings while they were young were told that their homosexuality was just a passing phase. Others find counseling from church leaders who are asking their congregations to imagine Christ saying, "Come unto me all ye unless you are gay or lesbian." They point out that nowhere in the Bible is there condemnation of loving, faithful relationships of any kind. Jesus refused to accommodate traditions that excluded whole groups of people, such as the Samaritans and the Gentiles.

Many religious organizations are beginning to address homophobia at national conferences and in individual synagogues and churches. While resistance is great, there is more awareness that as much as 5 percent of the people in a congregation may be hiding their sexual orientation.

Still, large numbers of conservatives and religious fundamentalists continue to believe that homosexuality is a sin. The leader of a campaign called "Save the Children" said, "God puts homosexuals in the same category as murderers."[5] During the Republican National Convention in Houston, Texas, in August 1992, television preacher Pat Robertson and conservative television commentator and politician Pat Buchanan made vehement attacks on homosexuals.[6]

Many religious leaders around the world disapprove strongly of same-sex activity, although they acknowledge that it has existed throughout history. Hindu religious texts frown on homosexual cult practices. Among Brahmins, members of the highest, or priestly, group of Hindus, homosexual acts are considered a source of pollution. A man might lose his caste (social position) for engaging in same-sex activity. Islam opposes homosexuality, but, despite the threat of a death penalty in Iran, it has been widely practiced in that Islamic country.[7]

Traditional Indian Buddhist teachings hold that homosexuality is basically genetic in origin, with the "same moral significance as heterosexuality." All expressions of sexuality are seen as impediments to spirituality. Sexual misconduct is to be avoided by homosexuals and heterosexuals. Rules for Buddhist monasteries are made in an effort to keep homosexual activity to a minimum, and the ordination of "sexually non-conforming males" is forbidden. However, certain orders, such as one of Mongolian monks, have justified homosexual relationships on religious grounds. In Japan, literature includes many references to homosexual activity in Buddhist monasteries between older monks and younger acolytes (boys who assist in the religious ceremonies).[8]

Feelings that homosexual relationships are morally wrong are quite common even among people who are not strongly religious. A poll that compared the reactions of American adults to homosexual relationships in 1992 to reactions expressed in 1978 showed only a slight change.[9] Still, homosexuals seem to be more accepted by the general public, especially by those who have learned to separate fact from fiction. For example, some general-interest bookstores and major book clubs are including a larger selection of titles about gays and lesbians.[10] In another example of increased acceptance, the National Gay and Lesbian

Law Association was allowed to become part of the American Bar Association in 1992.[11]

Admission of gays and lesbians to the armed forces has been a subject of controversy in many countries. In the United States, from 1943 to 1992, between 80,000 and 100,000 gays and lesbians were discharged from the military service because of their sexual orientation. A thousand gays were discharged after Operation Desert Storm in 1991.[12] Yet throughout this time homosexuals were permitted to serve in civilian jobs for the military, even at the highest and most sensitive levels. And by 1992, polls showed that most Americans believed homosexuals should be allowed in the military.[13]

In a review of the Pentagon's policy of banning homosexuals, investigators pointed out that the American Psychiatric Association and the American Psychological Association disagreed with the Defense Department's claim that a ban is necessary to ensure "good order, discipline and morale." A study done for the Pentagon a few years ago found that homosexuals were no more of a security risk than soldiers who were not gay.[14] But sentiment runs strong among those who are against allowing homosexuals to serve in the military. Over the centuries, arguments for barring them from the military have been strikingly similar to those used to bar blacks and women—but these barriers have fallen and opinions have changed.

In a television debate in the spring of 1992, an Air Force officer described gays as not being trustworthy because they live by deception. He claimed they would destroy the bonding, faith in one another, and trust that make a military unit.[15] Other military leaders pointed out that there would be no need for deception if the ban was lifted. They noted that many thousands of gays have served the armed forces well, some in responsible positions and with distinction.

Colonel Margarethe Cammermyer, a decorated Army nurse, was discharged from the Washington State Army National Guard in 1992 because she was a lesbian. Her case was one of several that received wide publicity and helped focus public attention on the armed forces policy. In another, Navy Petty Officer V. Keith Meinhold was discharged after making his homosexuality known on national television. Meinhold took the Navy to court, and a federal judge ruled in January 1993 that the military's policy was unconstitutional.

The ruling came in the middle of a controversy over President Bill Clinton's announcement, soon after taking office, that he would end the military ban. Although supporters of the ban moved to oppose him and delay the action, the United States was in fact one of only a handful of countries that barred homosexuals from military service. Of the sixteen countries who are members of NATO (North Atlantic Treaty Organization), all but Britain and the United States had lifted the ban by the end of 1992. In South Africa, draftees and permanent forces are not questioned about their sexuality, but recruits who appear to be openly homosexual may undergo a psychological examination and be dismissed. Soldiers in Japan who fail to maintain the military's dignity are subject to dismissal.

One reason for questioning the admission of

homosexuals to the military has been the fear of spreading AIDS. Those who oppose allowing gays to serve on the battlefield point out the possibility of the exchange of blood from a wounded man with AIDS to another individual. This argument is countered by the knowledge that transmission is unlikely when both blood and servicemen are tested routinely.

While many reasons were given for opposing the approval of homosexuals in the military, the controversy increased awareness that large numbers of homosexuals had always served in all of the armed forces. Many people, who think of homosexuals only in terms of their sexual behavior, and find it offensive, were upset by the idea of their being allowed to be open about their orientation. Others pointed out that bans against gays do not really discourage homosexuality; they encourage deceit.

In July 1993, President Clinton announced a policy that would allow homosexuals to serve in the military if they kept quiet about their sexual preferences and did not engage in homosexual behavior. Although military leaders supported the new policy, gay rights activists were deeply disappointed, while some conservatives were outraged that any change had been made in the ban.

Feelings run strong on many fronts beyond the military. Gays of all ages continue to be "bashed" and, in spite of some increase in understanding, many of them feel that they must hide their true sexual orientation until the general climate has changed.

▼ SIX ▼
GROWING UP GAY

Brian was tired of hearing his parents tell stories about the problems they had when they were growing up. They seemed to think he would appreciate their hardships and realize how lucky he was to be living now instead of then, but Brian knew that they could never begin to understand how he felt. They did not know he was gay, and he was still afraid to tell them.

While each heterosexual looks back on many experiences that were very personal and different from those of anyone else, each shares some common problems. The same is true for homosexuals. They grow up in a world that expects them to date the opposite sex, marry, and have children.

Mrs. Jones is typical of a mother who hated homosexuals, even after she had learned that her own daughter Eva was a lesbian. Mrs. Jones blamed herself for sending Eva to boarding school, where she believed lesbians recruited "innocent people" like her daughter. Mrs. Jones was unaware that Eva knew she had homosexual feelings while she was living at home.

Eva was afraid to tell her mother that she was a lesbian before she went away to school. Even after she joined a support group for gays, she spent many hours debating whether or not she should tell her mother about her sexual orientation. If she was part of a group of people who were trying to educate society to accept them, how could she keep her secret from her own mother? Maybe her mother would change her attitude and join Parents and Friends of Lesbians and Gays (P-FLAG), an organization supportive of parents of gay children. But Mrs. Jones continued to believe that Eva was living a life of sin. Eva felt better about herself after she came out of the closet, but her relationship with her mother was strained.

Although many heterosexuals grow up in families with single parents, the boy-girl tradition continues. Heterosexuals have many role models, from Adam and Eve to Romeo and Juliet to television shows and movies as well as members of their own families and their friends. No one knows how many men and women pretend to be heterosexual, marry, and have children in order to appear to fit in. Young people who are homosexual—an estimated 3 million in the United States—do not have these role models.[1]

The homosexuality of outstanding figures in history is not mentioned in the textbooks, and gay authors are not acknowledged as such. For example, did you learn that Richard the Lion-Hearted, Leonardo da Vinci, Michelangelo, Francis Bacon,

Walt Whitman, Tchaikovsky, and Herman Melville were homosexuals? The list of men and women of great talent who were homosexuals is long. The sexual orientation of present-day gay role models, such as tennis champions Billy Jean King, Martina Navratilova, and Bill Tilden; professional football running back Dave Kopay; Olympic gold-medal swimmer Bruce Hayes; writer Somerset Maugham, actor Rock Hudson; and politician Harvey Milk is often held against them. Some gays even join in making fun of homosexuals in their efforts to hide their own sexual orientation or confusion about their identity.

There is no set age at which a person becomes aware that he or she is homosexual. Some children feel different from their friends at an early age, with many becoming aware of their homosexuality during adolescence. Many adults who feel that they must be heterosexual because of social pressures do not realize their true sexual identity until after they are married and have started a family.

For Eric, the realization that he was homosexual came bit by bit. Although he was not interested in sports when he was very young, he became a good basketball player in high school, where he grew to be very tall. He dated some girls but he did not really enjoy himself. He hated the fact that his classmates called him "weirdo" and made fun of his voice and his walk.

Eric was a good basketball player in college, where he continued to pass for straight. However, he was always conscious of the conversations in the locker room about a teammate, Peter, who was gay. Eric was not about to admit his own sexual orientation and suffer the ridicule that he knew would follow his coming out, but he could not help feeling that he was being unfair to Peter. Maybe he should be doing something to make others understand that Peter was a sensitive, caring person. Peter did not choose his sexual orientation any more than Eric, or anyone else, did. It just happened.

One day Eric confided to Peter that he, too, was homosexual. He told him that he had known that he was different from other boys from the time he was twelve years old. The first time he heard the word "queer" was after a family friend committed suicide because he had AIDS. Eric's parents had gone to the funeral, and they remarked about the fact that the man's lover was asked to stand away from the family. He was not accepted, even though he had been the one who cared for their son in the difficult days before his death. The family did not invite the roommate to the reception after the funeral because they blamed him for their son's death. Others told them this was not true, but it did not help the parents to be more compassionate. Eric remembered feeling that this family was very cruel. He also remembered his parents saying that they understood why no one would want a "queer" mixing with "nice" people at the funeral.

Peter's childhood was very different from Eric's. Peter said that his parents were shocked when they learned he was gay, but they soon learned to accept him as he was. His mother had joined P-FLAG (Parents and Friends of Lesbians and Gays).

Eric wished his family could be more understanding. He told Peter about the year he decided that he really was gay. He had often thought he might be, but he was not sure for a long time. He hoped it was not true, for he had heard his brother ridicule gay boys in their school and tell ugly jokes about them. His brother used names such as fag, queer, lessie, and dyke for gay men and women even though he never would have said nigger, kike, wop, or mick for blacks, Jews, Italians, or Irish the way many people do. Eric's brother engaged in gay bashing, along with many of his friends. He had no idea that he was hurting his own brother.

As Eric grew older, he experienced some of the self-hate and low self-esteem that are common to many young homosexuals. He made friends with other boys, until they neglected him for some girl. He knew he liked boys as friends, and he felt sure he liked them sexually. All his sexual fantasies were about boys and older men. He had no interest in girls, except as friends.

Eric wanted to know more about homosexuality, but he was afraid to ask anyone he knew. So he went to the library for books on the subject of gays and lesbians. The one book that he found described gays as having many partners. These men met at gay bars, and had numerous brief encounters.

Eric tried meeting people at gay bars and he had brief affairs with many different gays. He enjoyed the sexual part of his evenings out, but he felt guilty lying to his family about where he was going. He also hated himself for being gay. He knew his brother would be ashamed of him and his parents might not even speak to him if they learned the truth.

Eric wished he knew some homosexuals who were more interesting than those strangers he picked up at the gay bars. He wanted to make friends with someone who shared his hobbies of music and reading, but when he was in high school, he did not find a person his own age, or even an older one, whom he could admire. If, as he had heard, one person in ten is homosexual, where were the more intellectual types? Were they afraid of losing their jobs if they admitted their sexual orientation?

Some of the gays who grew up around Eric were in hiding and some still are. But the climate in his neighborhood was changing. There were some support groups at churches, community centers, and even in some of the schools in another part of the city. Although Eric did not feel ready to join them, he was moving in this direction when he confided in Peter.

Even when he was the star of his basketball team, Eric still felt that he would never be able to live with someone in a long-term relationship. He wondered if he would ever be able to have a home with someone he loved. But all this changed as he grew closer to Peter. The two of them hoped to enjoy many years together in their own home.

Sara knew she was a lesbian before her sixteenth birthday, but she kept quiet about it. She had seen her classmates throw food at a gay in the cafeteria, and she heard the names they called him. One day, a boy was beaten just because he acted like a gay.

Sara felt that all homosexuals must be terrible people if others treated them so badly, but she knew she had to talk to someone about what was going on in her life. She could not trust her friends at school, and there was no guidance counselor who acted as if she would understand problems such as hers. Sara decided to confide in her mother. At first, she refused to believe Sara, then she called her a freak and told her to get out of the house.

If Sara's own mother could not accept her because she was a lesbian, how could she expect anyone else to like her? Sara's life seemed to fall completely apart. She was sure that she deserved the pain she felt, but she did not know where to go for help. After she left home, she discovered a hotline that led her to a shelter. At the shelter, workers talked with her day after day. They told her not to feel guilty about her feelings for other girls. They helped her understand that she was one of millions of people who are homosexuals.

Sara felt better about herself after many sessions of group therapy. The shelter arranged for her placement with a foster family in which the adults were both lesbians. She was able to finish school and apply for a part-time scholarship at the college of her choice.

Many young people are forced to leave home simply because they are gay or lesbian. Not every runaway, or "throwaway," is as lucky as Sara. Survival on the streets usually means earning money from illegal activities, including drug dealing and prostitution.

Growing up gay means grappling with the usual problems of adolescence coupled with discrimination, prejudice, feelings of loneliness and being different, and low self-esteem. Sometimes it means listening to family members degrade gays and lesbians. Sometimes the pain leads to substance abuse.

Many homosexuals of all ages hide their pain with excessive drinking or the use of illegal drugs. The rate of alcoholism among these groups has been estimated to be three times that of the general public.[2] Many studies show that a disproportionate number of homosexuals have problems with alcohol and other drugs.[3] About 6 percent of people with AIDS are both homosexual and drug users.[4] Homosexual drug abusers find special help in a number of places. For example, Pride Institute in Eden Prairie, Minnesota, provides treatment for gays and lesbians with chemical dependency.

Many young gays engage in heterosexual behavior in an effort to change their orientation. This often turns out to be a losing battle. One potentially serious consequence is pregnancy, which may occur accidentally or in an effort to "prove" heterosexual orientation.[5]

In addition to all the other problems, growing up gay today means learning to live with the fear, and sometimes the suffering, of AIDS. Many homosexuals are greatly concerned about whether or not they have had sexual contact with someone who carried HIV, the virus that causes AIDS. Since the incubation period of the virus can be ten or more years, such fears can haunt people over a long period of time.

Many people today are especially concerned about the spread of AIDS among young people.

According to the House Select Committee on Children, Youth and Families, at least 40,000 adolescents are newly infected with the AIDS virus each year. By the end of 1992, U.S. public health officials estimated 14.3 percent of gay and bisexual men under the age of twenty-four were infected by it.[6] Efforts to educate young people in safe sex practices are growing; but teens are known for their willingness to take risks. In a survey reported late in 1992, about 42 percent of teens said they would engage in sexual intercourse even if a condom were not available.[7]

Although awareness of the problems of growing up gay is growing, most young homosexuals suffer their fears and low self-esteem in silence. They are unknown victims of every homophobic remark they hear or assault they witness, and this makes them increasingly afraid to associate with others. The process that began with feelings of being different—sometimes several years before adolescence—too often ends with suicidal feelings or behavior.

Your help in separating myths from realities may mean a decrease in the amount of gay bashing by people who do not realize how their words hurt.

▼ SEVEN ▼
GAY AND LESBIAN FAMILIES

Two parents and two sets of children, three parents with one set of children, one parent with children, four parents with three sets of children . . . these are just a few of the kinds of families that are becoming common. The number of traditional families, one mother and one father with their own natural children, has been declining steadily. The traditional family has even been called an endangered species.

The number of unmarried people who are living together has increased to about 3 million of the 93 million households in the United States. This is five times as many unmarried couples as twenty years ago.[1] Some of these unmarried people have children and some do not, but they are often considered families.

While many individuals still insist that a real family consists of a mother, father, and their children, new definitions of a family are becoming more popular. In a recent survey, almost three quarters of the people polled said they thought of a family as a "group of people who love and care for each other," not as one in which the people are "related by blood, marriage, or adoption."[2]

Many people find it more difficult to consider gay and lesbian couples this way. Yet same-sex couples in long-term relationships are increasingly open about their sexual orientation and becoming more insistent about their desire to be considered a family. A number of companies and municipalities allow hospitalization and other benefits to these couples, just as they do to a husband and wife. Gays who wish to marry compare themselves with blacks who could not marry whites in one third of the states not so many years ago. But many individuals feel that gay marriage is too radical for society.

While not commonly recognized, the number of gay and lesbian families, with and without children, is growing. There are families in which one or two parents are homosexual. There may be children from a former marriage, adopted children, or natural children conceived through artificial insemination.

While the decline of the family has been deplored for over a hundred years, not everyone feels that the American family is losing its ability to carry out its functions of child raising and providing stability for adult life. The family as an institution may just be showing a larger variety of arrangements that fit with the modern age.[3]

Nontraditional families may be as stable as many traditional families, and some are more so. However, children in nontraditional families often have more problems while growing up. According to the National Commission on Children, children in single-parent families appear to be at greater risk than those in two-parent families for alcohol and other drug abuse, juvenile delinquency, dropping out of school, mental illness, adolescent pregnancy, and suicide. However, it is not fair to blame all of this on single parenting. Other factors, such as parents' level of education and employment can contribute to children being at risk.[4]

Many gay parents are especially aware of their need to do a good job with their children, so they work harder at good family relationships. Being a child in a gay home presents special challenges. How do you think you might feel if you were growing up in a home where one of your parents was gay? Perhaps you would be asked to keep a parent's homosexuality secret. Perhaps you would not even know about it. Or, if a parent was openly gay, you might suffer ridicule or even beatings from classmates. Still, many children of gay parents are well adjusted and proud of their parents.

Consider the feelings of a daughter of a lesbian who chose to write about her mother in a term paper. She begins by saying, "I wish I could tell people what my mother is like." She explains that she has a wonderful mother, but neighbors say mean things about her because they do not understand that lesbians can be good people.

"They talk about lack of family values, but they do many things that our family would consider immoral. For example, what is moral about beating my brother just because our mother is a lesbian?"

Many lesbian mothers would like to admit that they are gay, but they do not want to subject their children to the discrimination, name-calling, and hate that many straights would heap on them. Gays and lesbians can be good parents, and they can be bad parents. So can heterosexuals.

No one knows how many of the estimated 23 million gays and lesbians who live in the United States have formed families, or how many of these families include children. According to one estimate, about 6 percent of the population of the United States is made up of gay and lesbian families with children.[5] No one knows how many gays and lesbians have divorced the other parents of their children and left the original families after they became aware of their sexual orientation. In many cases, lesbians continue to raise their children after the divorce.

There are probably many parents who quietly leave their heterosexual partners for lovers of the same sex, when they realize their sexual orientation after they are married. In some cases, their spouses and children are accepting, and in some, they are not.

Since most of society disapproves of same-sex couples raising children, many who do so live under tremendous stress. They often join support groups. There are as many as thirty-five chapters of gay parents' organizations in the United States. In some cities, counseling groups for children of gay parents have formed.[6]

Studies show that some of the most helpful behaviors for lesbian mothers include talking to others in the same situation, socializing with lesbian friends, and building close relationships. Not revealing lesbian identity was found to be among the least helpful behaviors.[7]

Most three-parent families include a mother, father, and a step-parent, but there are some in which two lesbians raise a child that was born to one of them after conception by artificial insemination.

Sometimes a divorced parent of a traditional marriage asks the court to forbid visitation rights with a homosexual parent while his or her partner is present. Many gay parents hope that their spouses will allow them to continue a close relationship with their children. Young children are often unaware or accepting of a gay parent's sexual orientation. When children are older, some are upset about it, although they may continue to enjoy visits at the gay parent's home. If a father or his lover develops AIDS, the situation can become more complicated. Mothers then tend to be concerned that the children will be infected and may forbid them to visit even though AIDS can only be spread by exchange of body fluids. There have been cases in which mothers objected to friendship with the father's partner even if he was healthy; but when AIDS is involved, fear of infection can become a major problem.

The parents of gays often have a difficult time accepting their children's lovers. When a son or daughter becomes very ill or disabled, these parents seldom include the lovers in family decisions, even though that person has been a good caregiver. Karen Thompson is a lesbian who took care of her partner, Sharon Kowalski, for several years after she was paralyzed by an automobile accident. When Sharon Kowalski's parents discovered the lesbian relationship, they moved her to a distant nursing home and refused visiting rights for Karen Thompson. After a seven-year court battle, Thompson was awarded legal guardianship of Kowalski, something that would have been automatically granted to a heterosexual spouse.[8]

Although lesbian and gay families often have difficulty in being accepted by other family members and by neighbors, they are making some progress. An estimated one third of lesbians have children, either from former marriages or by artificial insemination.[9] Adoption by gay singles or couples is also gaining acceptance. Many gay couples, both male and female, provide loving, caring environments for children, sharing the care of the children.

Courts do not always rule in favor of homosexuals, even when two of them want to be the legal parents of a child. In February 1992, a six-year-old boy was legally adopted by his natural mother's partner in what was believed to be the first such adoption ever approved in New York State. The judge noted that there was no ruling that required adoptive parents to be of any particular gender. He noted that a child who receives proper physical care along with love and nurture from even a single parent can be counted among the blessed. In this case, the child had two adults dedicated to his welfare, secure in their loving relationship and determined to raise the child to the best of their abilities.[10]

This ruling is a far cry from the days when

people believed that homosexuals were agents of the devil and wreckers of family life, but some children who live in gay homes still suffer from the verbal and physical violence of people who dislike all homosexuals.

Adoptions by homosexuals can still be difficult and complicated, and foster parents may be disqualified if a member of the family is gay. This happened to a family in New Hampshire who had a large house in the country where they raised their own five children. Harold and Betsy Janeway, who were aware of the need for homes for foster children, applied to bring some to their home. One of the questions in the application asked if anyone in their home was homosexual. Two of their children, who were grown and lived in California, fitted the definition. When the Janeways made it clear that these children would always be welcome in their home, their application to care for foster children was denied. They were told that they would have to guarantee that their gay children would not come home or would come home for only short visits. In the application, gayness was defined by sex acts, a definition that irritates many knowledgeable people.[11]

However, many nontraditional parents succeed in reaching out to children who need homes, and new policies are helping to place foster children with them. For example, in 1990, Massachusetts acted to permit homosexual foster parents.

Families in which gays and lesbians admit their sexual orientation are expected to continue to increase as more members of this group fight against the prejudice they have known for years.

Today gays and lesbians face new pressures and challenges. AIDS, which has affected the gay community deeply, is among the greatest problems. Another is the continued effort for acceptance in mainstream society—an effort that has at times been met positively and at times negatively.

Ever since the first cases were diagnosed in 1981, AIDS has been an emotionally charged subject because the patients were homosexuals. Years after the discovery of the virus HIV (human immunodeficiency virus), which destroys the immune system and makes the body vulnerable to various other infections, AIDS was often called the gay plague. To some, the virus was not to blame; homosexuals were. "God's punishment for immoral behavior" was the common explanation offered by these people.

Although lesbians have the lowest rate of infection, and although the disease has spread to many heterosexuals through blood transfusions, sexual contact, and drug abuse, AIDS still means gay to many people. Certainly, the rate of HIV infection among homosexuals is high in the United States. In some countries, AIDS is more prevalent among heterosexuals, but in the United States, about 60% of the cases are found in gays. The Centers for Disease Control and Prevention reports that 142,626 men who had sex with men developed AIDS by the end of 1992.[1] Not all cases are reported.

Homosexuals, who had seldom been in the news, made the headlines often during the first decade after the discovery of AIDS. Information about gays and lesbians began reaching young people in schools and the public in general. Many myths were seen for what they were, and some progress was made in replacing them with facts.

Although gays were in the news, however, much of the news was sad. Today, many gay men over the age of thirty-five have lost a dozen to a hundred friends to the disease. Concern about possible infection is widespread. Blood tests can reveal the presence of infection with HIV; when results are positive, some manage to stave off illness for a while with medical care and early drug treatment. But early drug treatment can cost thousands of dollars a year and is unaffordable for many people. Many infected people do not qualify for government help until they are so sick that they are disabled.

The seriousness of AIDS and the large numbers of gays who have died or are dying from it have had a profound effect on the homosexual community. Gays and lesbians have led the effort to spread information about how the disease is transmitted. Now and then a homosexual makes headlines because of irresponsible behavior in spreading AIDS, but these cases are the exception. Even some of the most homophobic individuals are willing to admit that homosexuals should be praised for the way they have educated each other about how AIDS is spread.

Many homosexuals have banded together to help not only each other but all people with AIDS. Their help with babies born infected with the disease is well known. Through some organizations, volunteers have acted as "buddies" to people with AIDS. After the lovers and friends they cared for have died, these volunteers have kept house, listened to problems, and helped other people with AIDS in many different ways. This kind of caring by both homosexual and heterosexual volunteers continues, but there are never enough caregivers or hospital beds.

The government's early denial of the seriousness of the newest major public health problem brought many homosexuals out of the closet. They joined in the plea for faster action in medical research and pharmaceutical laboratories. Opinions about what was done to fight and prevent AIDS vary from praise for tremendous effort on the part of the scientific community to complaints about lack of funding and denial by the government. Activist groups such as ACT UP, which was organized in 1987 to work for more and faster action, are themselves controversial. Many heterosexuals see them as too militant. Both homosexuals and heterosexuals suggest that such groups may be increasing hostility against gays. Others commend their aggressive actions, believing that these groups have helped to make the government move faster in its quest for new drugs and vaccines. Certainly, stopping the AIDS virus remains a challenge that has not been conquered.

The AIDS crisis has forced educators to deal with subjects that were once taboo. Since the newest wave of AIDS cases is expected to come from today's teens, education of the young must play a major role in prevention.

In areas as different as educating young people about AIDS and the development of tolerance for everyone, controversy arises when homosexuality is mentioned. Sex education has always been a sensitive issue, and same-sex love is especially so. Attitudes about gays and lesbians often leave no room for moderation. One example of a problem with teaching tolerance could be seen in New York City in 1992, when some elementary school teachers balked at a teaching guide that urged them to provide classroom experiences that presented lesbians and gays as people to be appreciated and respected.[2] However, sexual practices are now discussed more openly than a decade ago in both schools and in the media.

The tragedy of AIDS and efforts to provide information about homosexuality have caused a backlash in some communities. In the 1992 presidential election, antigay measures were on the ballots in several states. Oregon voters defeated a ballot measure that denounced homosexuality as "abnormal" and perverse and would have required state and local governments to take steps to discourage homosexuality. In Portland, Maine, voters rejected an attempt to repeal local antidiscrimination laws that specifically protect homosexuals, but voters in Tampa, Florida, did repeal a similar law. Some of the arguments over this issue centered on a belief that homosexuals were asking for special protection.[3] In Colorado, voters approved a measure designed to strip away legal protection for gays. At least twenty-three hate crimes were reported almost immediately after the election, along with a general increase in gay bashing and angry protests by gays.[4]

While the political dawn seems to have arrived for gays in some localities, strong antigay feelings continue to be voiced in many places. Most gay policemen are still hiding their sexual orientation, but openly gay policemen serve throughout the department in New York City. As the military moved closer to official tolerance of homosexuals, new gay organizations came into being. One, begun late in 1992, was an association of alumni from West Point, a group that never would have come forward a few years earlier.[5]

Harvey Milk High, a gay high school in New York City; gay pride parades; and openly gay groups in many churches are a few signs of increased tolerance. There is a small increase in the number of companies that recognize gay partners in health-care programs. As of early 1993, eight states and about 135 localities protected gays against discrimination. Gays and lesbians held high positions in the Clinton administration. But violence, harassment, and discrimination continue on many fronts. To draw attention to this, hundreds of thousands of gays and lesbians and their supporters rallied in Washington, D.C., on April 25, 1993.

Gay rights activists predict that Congress will pass a law within ten years that will confer protection against discrimination in employment, housing, and public accommodations, something ethnic and racial minorities already have. They hope that the future will be better for all gays and lesbians, but it is predicted that many will continue to hide their sexual orientation. Much of the public wishes they would.

As the struggle for acceptance reaches a new and uncertain phase, many homosexuals vow to move forward in their fight for dignity. Knowing about homosexuality is just a beginning.

▼ SOURCE NOTES ▼

CHAPTER ONE

1. Richard R. Trioden in *Homosexuality: Research Implications for Public Policy* (Newbury Park, CA: Sage, 1991), p. 47.
2. Morton Hunt, *Gay: What Teenagers Should Know About Homosexuality and the AIDS Crisis* (New York: Farrar, Straus & Giroux, 1987), p. 9.
3. June M. Reinisch, *The Kinsey Institute New Report on Sex* (New York: St. Martin's Press, 1990), pp. 139–140.
4. Alex Thio, *Deviant Behavior* (Boston: Houghton Mifflin, 1987), p. 9.
5. Boston Women's Health Collective, *The New Our Bodies, Ourselves* (New York: Simon and Schuster, 1976), p. 149.
6. *New Haven Register*, October 8, 1991.
7. *The New York Times*, November 12, 1992.
8. Dana Finnegan and Emily B. McNally, *Dual Identities* (Center City, MN: Hazeldon, 1987), pp. 32–33.

9. John C. Gonsiorek and James D. Weinrich, *Homosexuality: Research Implications for Public Policy* (Newbury Park, CA: Sage, 1991), pp. 11–12.
10. Gilbert Herdt, editor, *Gay and Lesbian Youth* (Binghamton, NY: Harrington Park Press, 1989), p.2.
11. Report of the Secretary's Task Force on Youth Suicide, January 1989, Vol. 3, p. 111.

CHAPTER TWO

1. Vern L. Bullough and Bonnie Bullough, *Sin, Sickness, and Sanity: A History of Sexual Attitudes* (New York: Garland, 1977), p. 2.
2. Vern L. Bullough, *Homosexuality: A History* (New York: The New American Library, 1979), p. 53.
3. Martin Duberman, *About Time: Exploring the Gay Past* (New York: Penguin, 1991), p. 440.
4. David F. Greenberg, *The Construction of Homosexuality* (Chicago: The University of Chicago Press, 1988), p. 144.
5. Ibid., p. 33
6. David M. Halperin, *One Hundred Years of Homosexuality* (New York: Routledge, 1990), p. 22.
7. Greenberg, p. 124.
8. Richard A. Isay, *Being Homosexual: Gay Men and Their Development* (New York: Farrar, Straus & Giroux, 1989), p. 13.
9. Greenberg, p. 28.
10. Ibid., pp. 40–56.
11. Ibid., p. 202.
12. Duberman, p. 377.
13. Greenberg, pp. 302–323.
14. Martin Bauml Duberman, Martha Vicinus, and George Chauncey, Jr., editors, *Hidden from History: Reclaiming the Gay and Lesbian Past* (New York: New American Library, 1989), pp. 67–75.
15. Ibid., pp. 129–140, and Barry D. Adam, *The Rise of a*

Gay and Lesbian Movement (Boston: Twayne, 1987), pp. 6–8.

CHAPTER THREE

1. Vern L. Bullough and Bonnie Bullough, *Sin, Sickness and Sanity: A History of Sexual Attitudes* (New York: Garland, 1977), p. 11.
2. David F. Greenberg, *The Construction of Homosexuality* (Chicago: The University of Chicago Press, 1988), pp. 387–433.
3. Martin Duberman, *About Time: Exploring the Gay Past* (New York: Penguin, 1991), pp. 442–443.
4. Martin Bauml Duberman, Martha Vicinus, and George Chauncey, Jr., editors, *Hidden From History: Reclaiming the Gay and Lesbian Past* (New York: New American Library, 1989), pp. 294–317.
5. Barry D. Adam, *The Rise of a Gay and Lesbian Movement* (Boston: Twayne, 1987), p. 43.
6. Ibid., p. 44.
7. Duberman, Vicinus, and Chauncey, pp. 365–369.
8. Bullough, p. 67.

CHAPTER FOUR

1. Kenneth Lewis, *The Psychoanalytical Theory of Homosexuality* (New York: Simon and Schuster, 1988).
2. John Money, *Love and Love Sickness* (Baltimore: The Johns Hopkins Press, 1980), p. 87.
3. Richard A. Isay, *Being Homosexual: Gay Men and Their Development* (New York: Farrar, Straus, & Giroux, 1989), pp. 32–43.
4. June M. Reinisch, *The Kinsey Institute New Report on Sex* (New York: St. Martin's Press, 1990), p. 141.
5. Morton Hunt, *Gay: What Teenagers Should Know About Homosexuality and the AIDS Crisis* (New York: Farrar, Straus & Giroux, 1987), pp. 47–48.

6. *Science News*, August 22, 1992, p. 117.
7. *Peninsula*, October/November 1991, Vol. 3, Number 2, p. 2.
8. Hunt, p. 176.
9. *Science News*, January 4, 1992, Vol. 141, p. 6, and *Harvard Mental Health Letter*, Vol. 8. No. 12, June 1992.
10. *US News and World Report*, September 9, 1991, p. 58.

CHAPTER FIVE

1. *The New York Times*, June 4, 1992.
2. James E. Childress and John Macquarrie, *The Westminster Dictionary of Christian Ethics* (Philadelphia: Westminster Press, 1986), p. 274.
3. Ibid., p. 262.
4. *The New York Times*, June 11, 1992.
5. Ann Thomson Cook, *And God Loves Each One* (Washington, D.C.: Dumbarton Methodist Church, 1988, 1990).
6. *The New York Times Magazine*, October 11, 1992, p. 20.
7. David F. Greenberg, *The Construction of Homosexuality* (Chicago: University of Chicago Press, 1988), p. 100.
8. José Ignacio Cabezón, *Buddhism, Sexuality, and Gender* (Albany, NY: State University of New York Press, 1992), pp. 203–230.
9. *Time*, June 22, 1992, p. 21.
10. *The New York Times*, July 6, 1992.
11. *The New York Times*, August 12, 1992.
12. *Time*, August 19, 1991, pp. 14 and 17.
13. *The New York Times*, September 1, 1991.
14. *The New York Times*, June 20, 1992.
15. CNN Telecast, May 25, 1992.

CHAPTER SIX

1. Gilbert Herdt, editor, *Gay and Lesbian Youth* (New York: Harrington Park Press, 1989), p. xiv.

2. Sheppard B. Kominars, *Accepting Ourselves* (San Francisco: HarperSanFrancisco, 1989), p. xi.
3. Joseph Neisen and Hillary Sandall, "Alcohol and Other Drug Abuse in Gay/Lesbian Populations," *Journal of Psychology and Human Sexuality*, Vol. 3, No 1, 1990, p. 153.
4. Centers for Disease Control and Prevention, Atlanta, Georgia.
5. U.S. Department of Health and Human Services, *Report of the Secretary's Task Force on Youth Suicide*, Vol. 3 (Washington, D.C.: Superintendent of Documents, 1989), pp. 116 and 118.
6. *The New York Times*, November 30, 1992.
7. CDC, 1992.

CHAPTER SEVEN

1. *Newsweek*, March 23, 1992, pp. 62–63.
2. Ibid., p. 63.
3. *Psychology Today*, May/June 1992, pp. 32–37.
4. *US News and World Report*, June 8, 1992.
5. Editorial, *The New York Times*, September 28, 1992.
6. *Newsweek*, July 6, 1992, p. 62.
7. *Brown University Family Therapy Letter*, Vol. 4, No. 4, April 1992, p. 1.
8. *The New York Times*, December 18, 1991.
9. *Newsweek*, March 12, 1992, p. 24.
10. *The New York Times*, February 4, 1992.
11. *P-FLAGpole*, Summer 1992, p. 5.

CHAPTER EIGHT

1. Centers for Disease Control and Prevention, 1992.
2. *The New York Times*, November 17, 1992.
3. *The New York Times*, November 5, 1992.
4. *Newsweek*, November 23, 1992, p. 26.
5. *The New York Times*, December 1, 1992.

▼ FOR FURTHER INFORMATION ▼

RECOMMENDED READING

Alyson, Sasha, editor. *Young, Gay, and Proud.* Boston: Alyson Publications, 1980, 1985, 1991.

Cohen, Susan and Daniel Cohen. *When Someone You Know Is Gay.* New York: M. Evans and Company, 1989.

D'Emilio, John, and Estelle B. Freedman. *Intimate Matters: A History of Sexuality in America.* New York: Harper and Row, 1988.

Dudley, William, editor. *Homosexuality: Opposing Viewpoints.* San Diego, CA: Greenhaven, 1993.

Finnegan, Dana, and Emily McNally. *Dual Identities.* Center City, MN: Hazeldon, 1988.

Fricke, Aarin. *Reflections of a Rock Lobster: A Story About Growing Up Gay.* Boston: Alyson Publications, 1981.

Hankel, Frances, and Cunningham, John. *A Way of Love, A Way of Life: A Young Person's Introduction to What It Means to Be Gay.* New York: Lothrop, 1979.

Herdt, Gilbert, editor. *Gay and Lesbian Youth.* Binghamton, NY: Harrington Park Press, 1989.

Heron, Ann, and Meredith Maran. *How Would You Feel If Your Dad Was Gay?* Boston: Alyson, 1991.

Hilton, Bruce. *Can Homophobia Be Cured?* Nashville: Abingdon Press, 1992.

Hunt, Morton. *Gay: What You Should Know About Homosexuality.* New York: Farrar, Straus & Giroux, 1977.

Hyde, Margaret O., and Elizabeth Forsyth. *AIDS: What Does It Mean to You?*, 4th ed. New York: Walker and Company, 1992.

Isay, Richard. *Being Homosexual: Gay Men and Their Development.* New York: Farrar, Straus & Giroux, 1989.

Klein, Norma. *Now That You Know.* New York: Bantam Books, 1988.

Kominars, Sheppard B. *Accepting Ourselves.* San Francisco: HarperSanFrancisco, 1989.

Landau, Elaine. *Different Drummer: Homosexuality in America.* New York: Julian Messner, 1986.

Reinisch, June M. *The Kinsey Institute New Report on Sex: What You Must Know to Be Sexually Literate.* New York: St. Martins's Press, 1990.

Rench, Janice. *Understanding Sexual Identity.* Minneapolis, MN: Lerner, 1990.

Rose, A. L. *Homosexuals in History: A Study of Ambivalence in Society, Literature and the Arts.* New York: Dorset Press, 1977.

Tessina, Tina. *Gay Relationships.* Los Angeles: Jeremy T. Tarcher, Inc., 1989.

ORGANIZATIONS

Bienestar: Gay and Lesbian Latinos Unidos:
213-660-9680

Exodus International:
  Box 2121, San Rafael, CA 94912 (write)

Gay Men's Health Crisis:
  212-807-6655 (Hearing Impaired: 212-645-7470)

Homosexuals Anonymous Fellowship Services:
  215-376-1146

IYG Gay/Lesbian Youth Hotline:
  1-800-347-TEEN

Lambda Legal Defense and Education Fund, Inc.
  212-995-8585

National Gay and Lesbian Task Force:
  202-332-6483

National Runaway Switchboard—24 hour hotline:
  1-800-621-4000

National Youth Crisis Hotline:
  1-800-448-4663

FOR INFORMATION ABOUT AIDS

Centers for Disease Control and Prevention:
  operates 1-800-342-AIDS, 24 hours a day, 7 days a week

Hearing impaired:
  (TDD)-1-800-243-7889 operates 10:00 A.M. to 10:00 P.M.
  Eastern Time, Monday through Friday

Spanish language:
  1-800-344-SIDA, operates 8:00 A.M. to 2:00 A.M.
  Eastern Time, 7 days a week

Other sources of information about AIDS

Aids Hotline for Teens:
  1-800-234-TEEN
  (staffed by trained high school students)

American National Red Cross:
1-800-26-BLOOD

Centers for Disease Control and Prevention
AIDS Information Office:
404-329-2891

National AIDS Information Clearinghouse:
1-800-458-5231

National Association of People with AIDS:
1-800-338-AIDS

National Institute of Allergy and Infectious Diseases:
1-800-TRIALS-A

National Native American AIDS Prevention Center:
1-800-283-AIDS

The Pediatric AIDS Foundation:
1-213-395-9051

Look under the following headings in the Yellow Pages of your telephone book for further help in locating organizations that provide information about gays, lesbians, and AIDS: Clinics, Social and Human Services, Counseling.

If you would like a current list of community resources throughout the United States, write to Lambda Youth Network, P.O. Box 7911, Culver, CA 90233. Their resource list includes pen-pal programs, talklines, newsletters, handouts, and bibliographies for young gays, lesbians, and bisexuals. Send a self-addressed, stamped envelope and include a donation of a dollar.

▼ INDEX ▼